Sharks

Written by John Chandler

Illustrated by Donald Gates

What are sharks like?
What do sharks do?

Sharks are fish. They live in the sea.

There are many different kinds of sharks.
Some are very small. Some are very large.

That's a cat shark. It's small. It's as long
as your arm.

That's a tiger shark. It's as long as a car.

Tiger sharks need to eat a lot.

The whale shark is the largest shark in the sea.

8

It's as big as two elephants.

Sharks are always looking for food.

They look and listen. They can feel the water
move when other fish swim by.

Sharks eat other fish and sea animals.

Look at those teeth!

Sharks have rows and rows of very sharp teeth.
If they break a tooth, they grow a new one!

Most sharks will not harm people, but some sharks do.

So it's hard to get near sharks.

How do you know so much about sharks?

That's my mom.